I0006654

THIS BUSINESS ANALYST'S NOTEBOOK JOURNAL BELONGS TO:

_____

_____

_____

_____

_____

_____

✸

OBJECTIVE

_____

_____

_____

_____

PROJECT

_____

_____

_____

_____

www.ingramcontent.com/pod-product-compliance
Lightning Source LLC
Chambersburg PA
CBHW051244050326
40689CB00007B/1057

* 9 7 8 1 0 9 8 7 3 1 6 4 9 *